**THE COLORS THAT
EMBELLISH THE PAGES OF
THIS BOOK WERE HAND
PICKED AND METICULOUSLY
APPLIED BY**

_____

COPYRIGHT 2020
AUTHOR & ILLUSTRATOR DIEGO EL-AMIN
www.cubedmotif.com

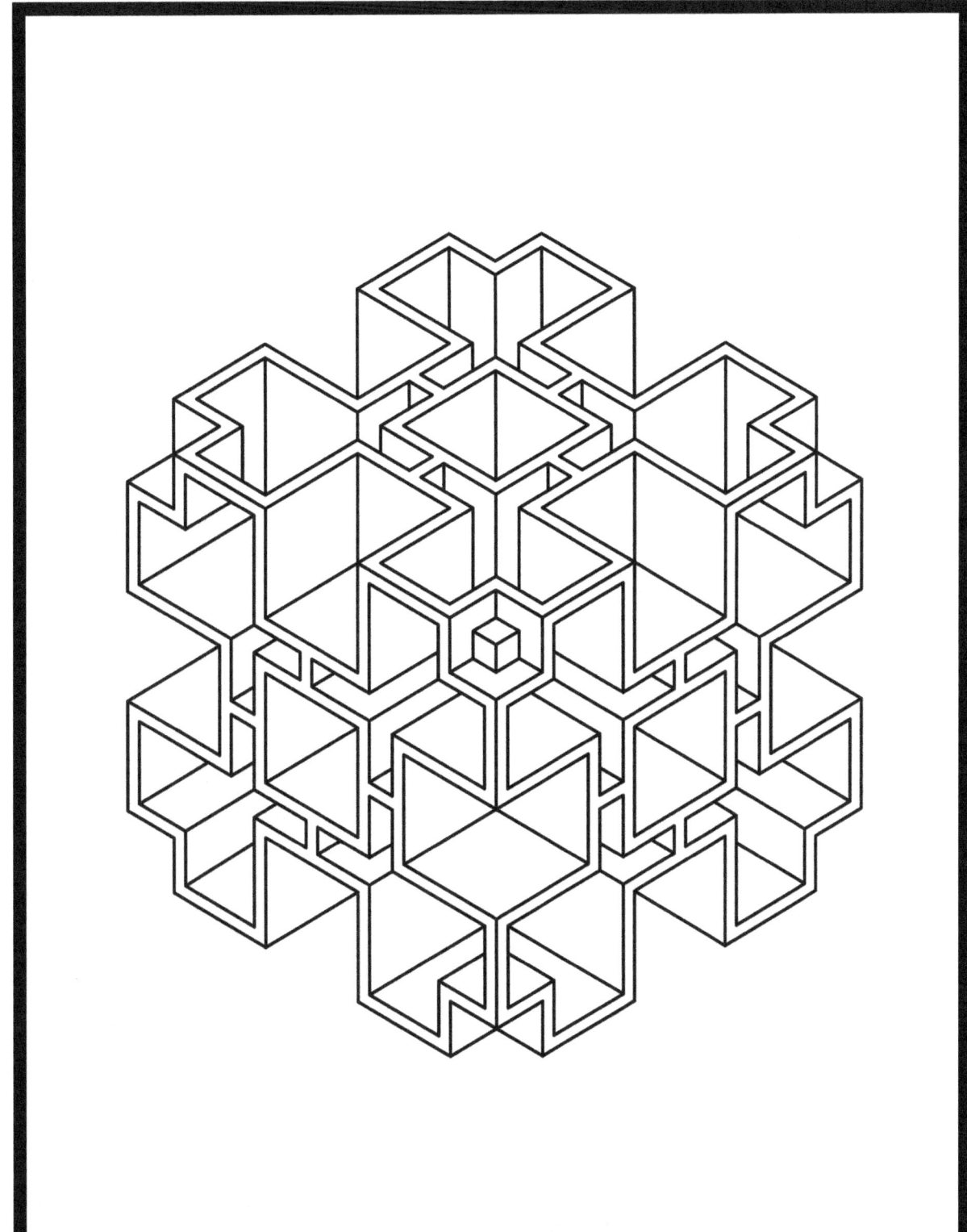

Cube No. 1

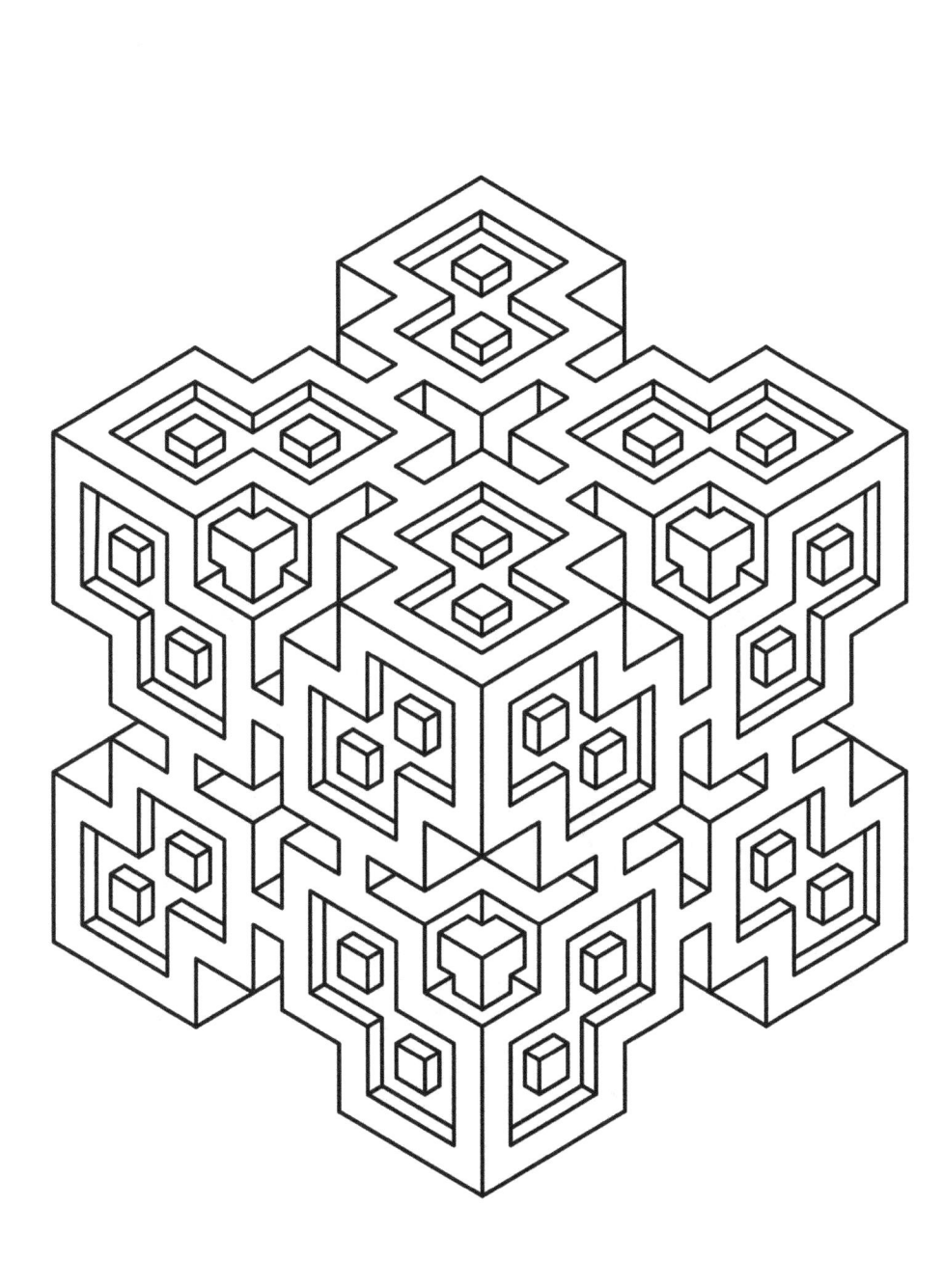

Cube No. 2

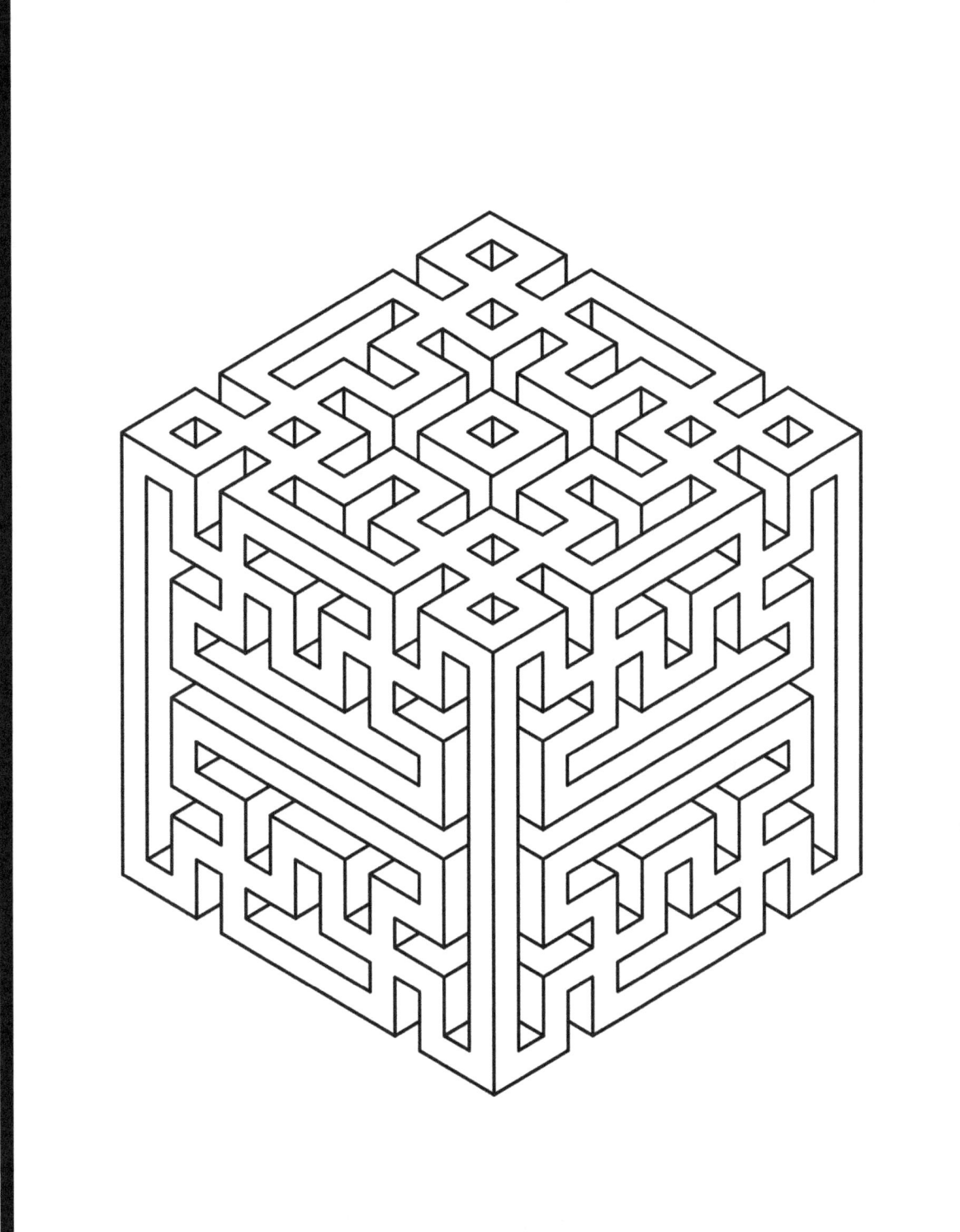

Cube No. 3

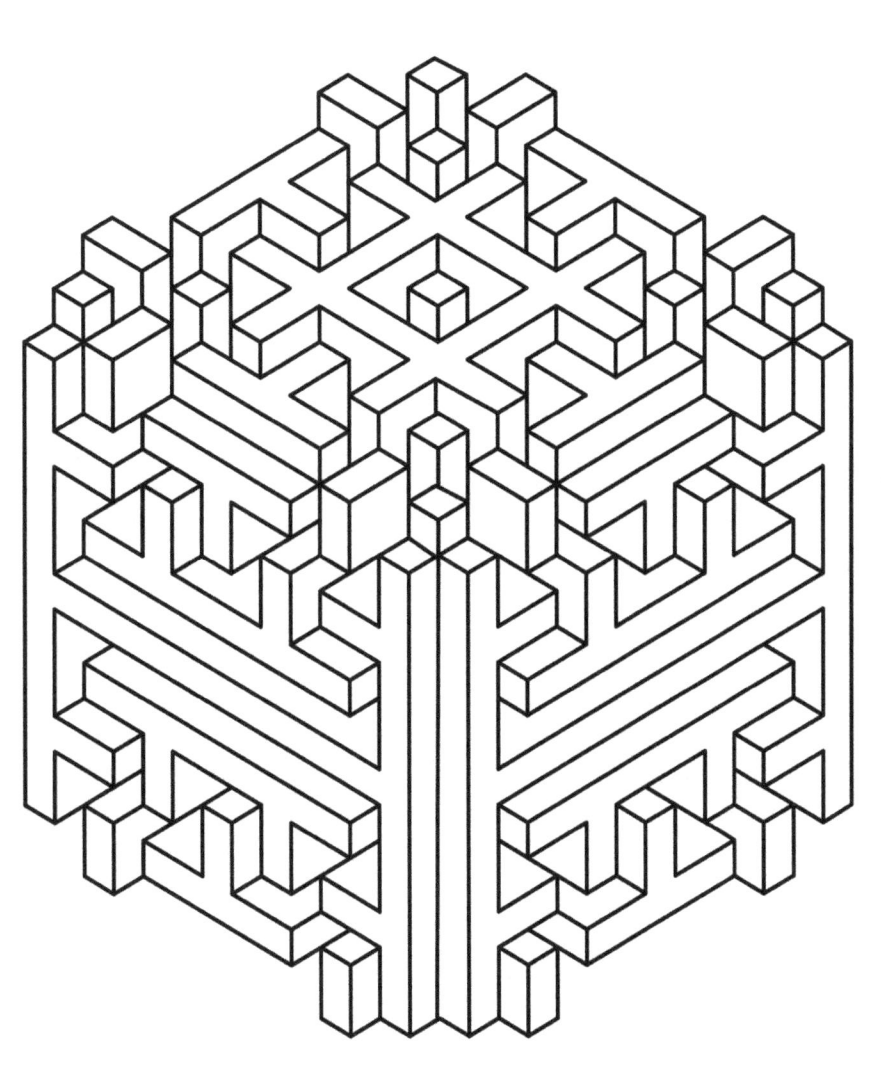

Cube No. 4

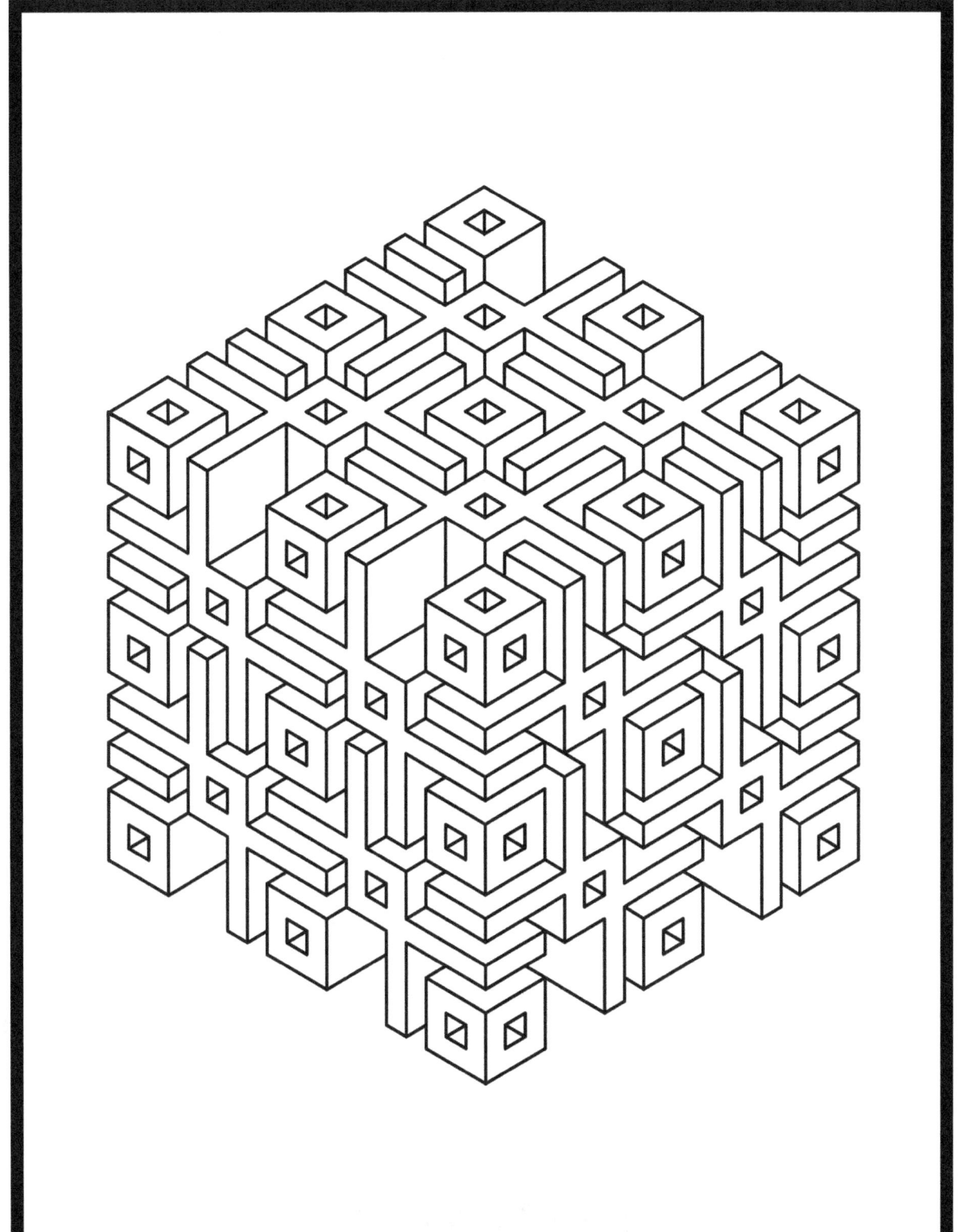

Cube No. 5

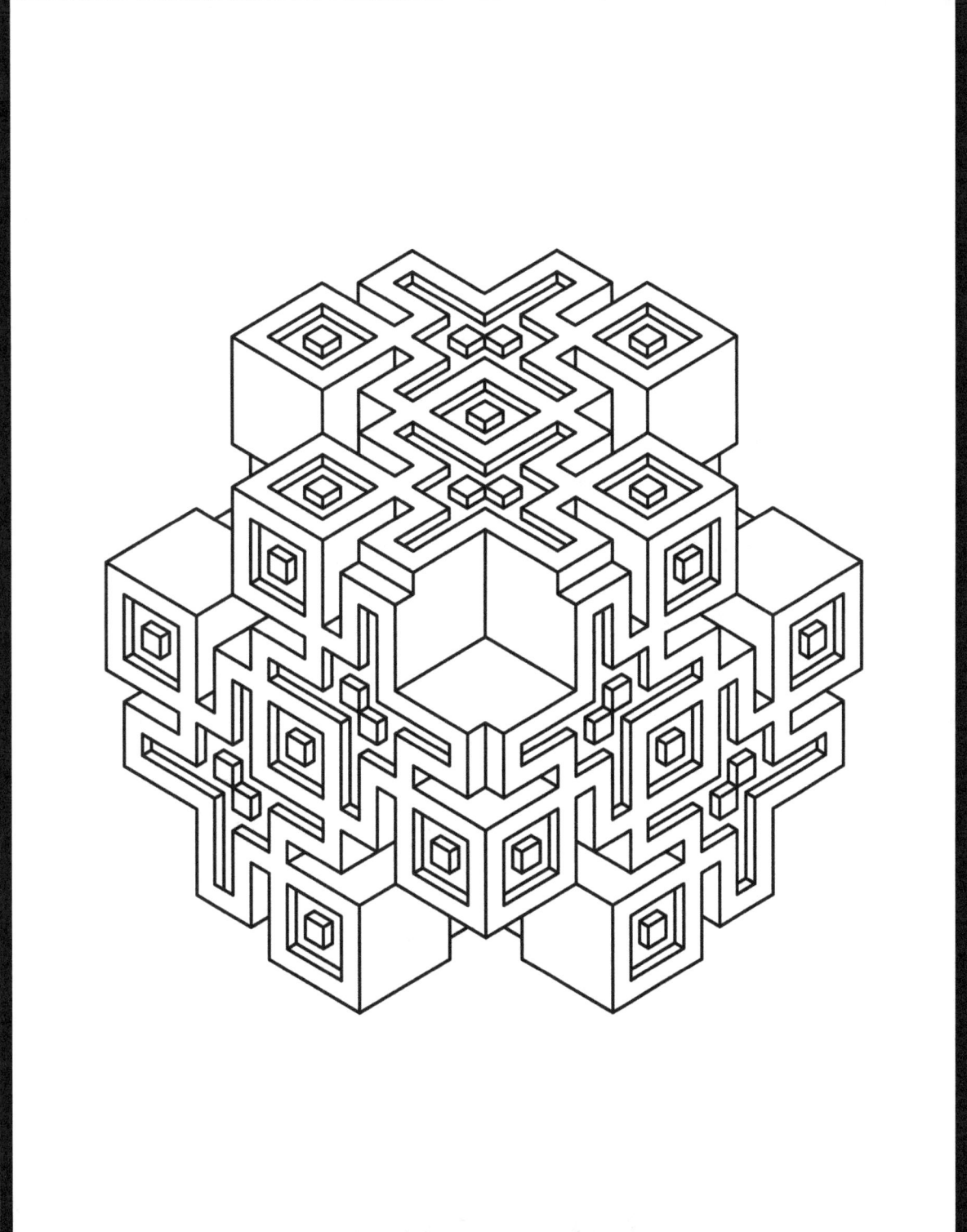

Cube No. 6

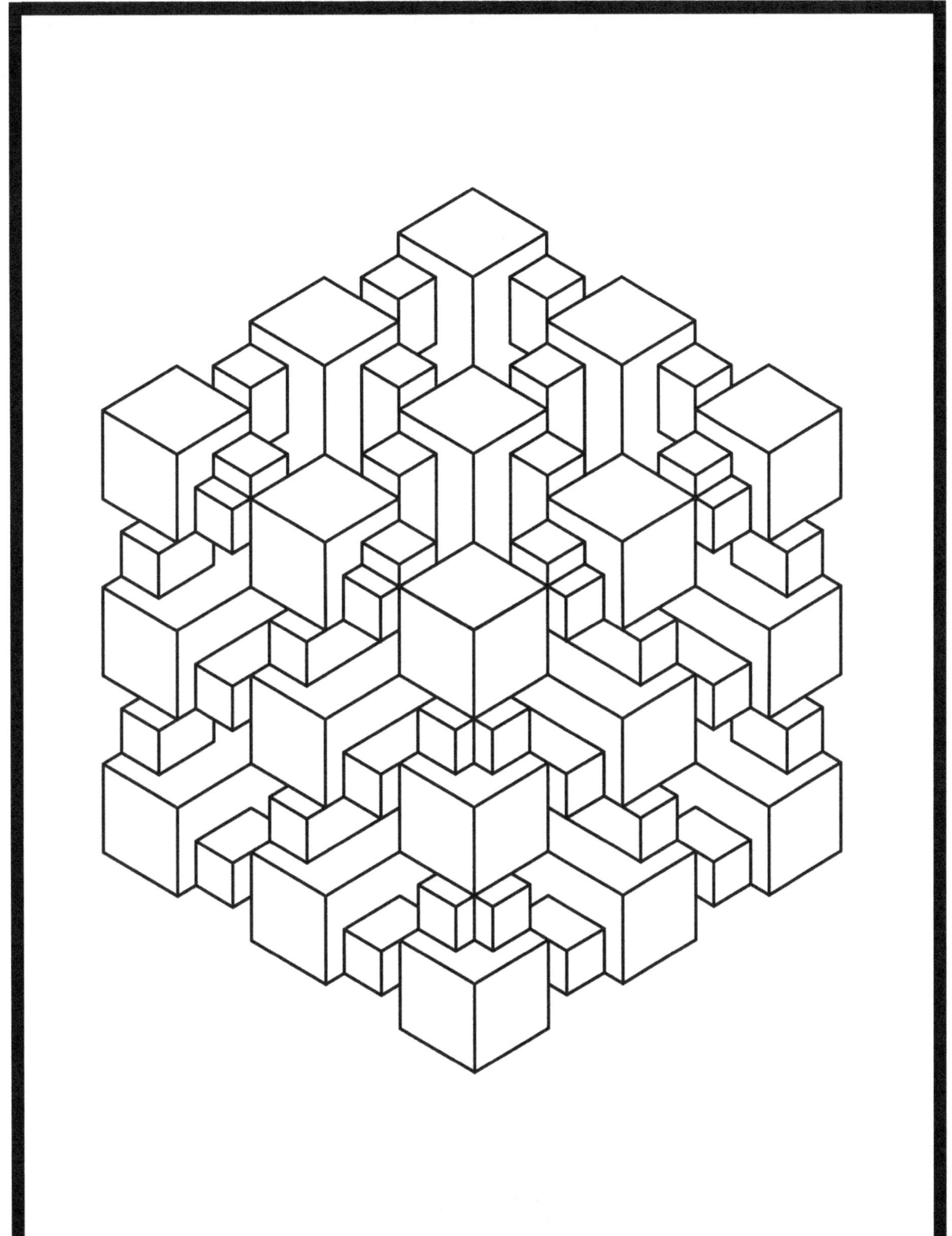

Cube No. 7

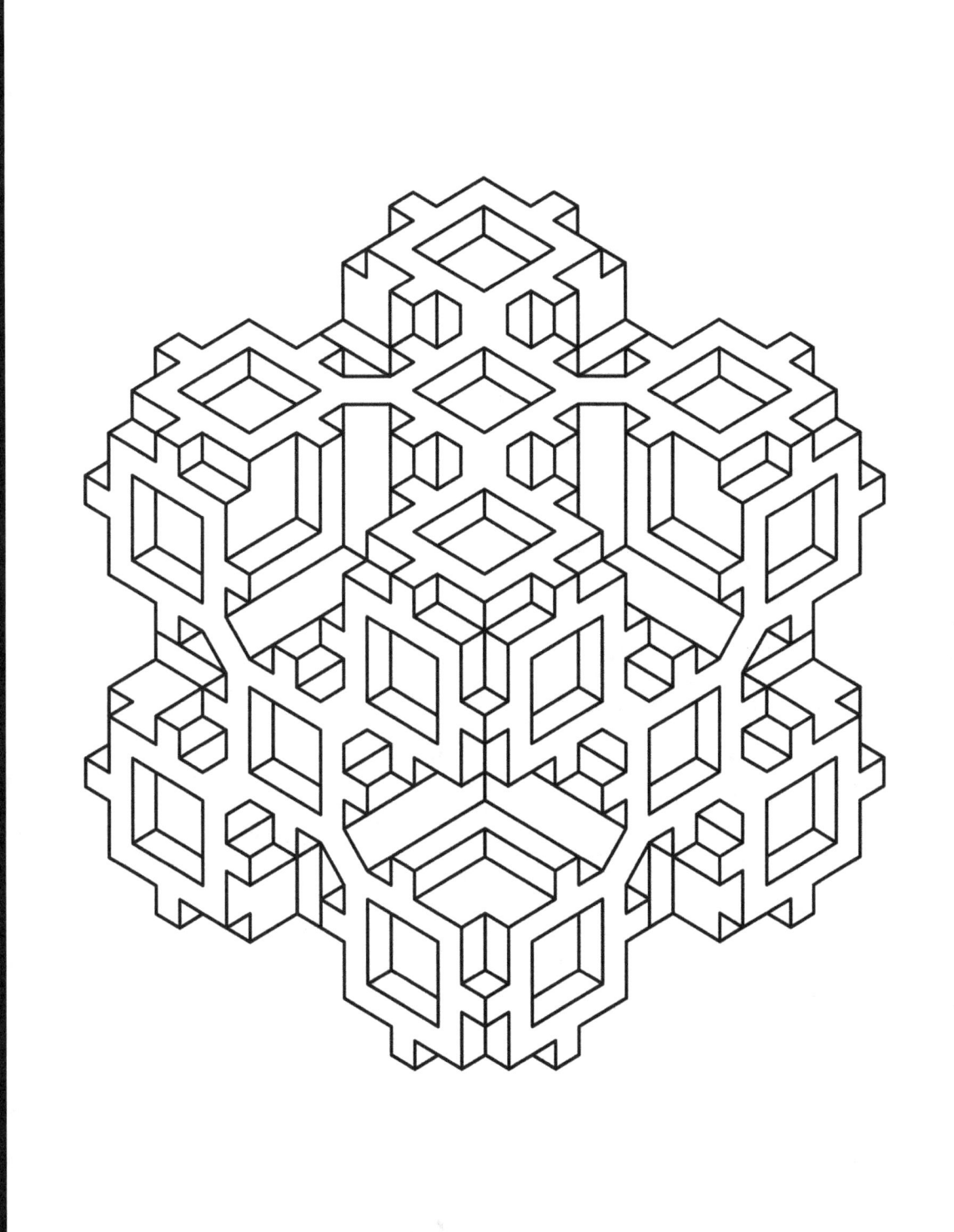

Cube No. 8

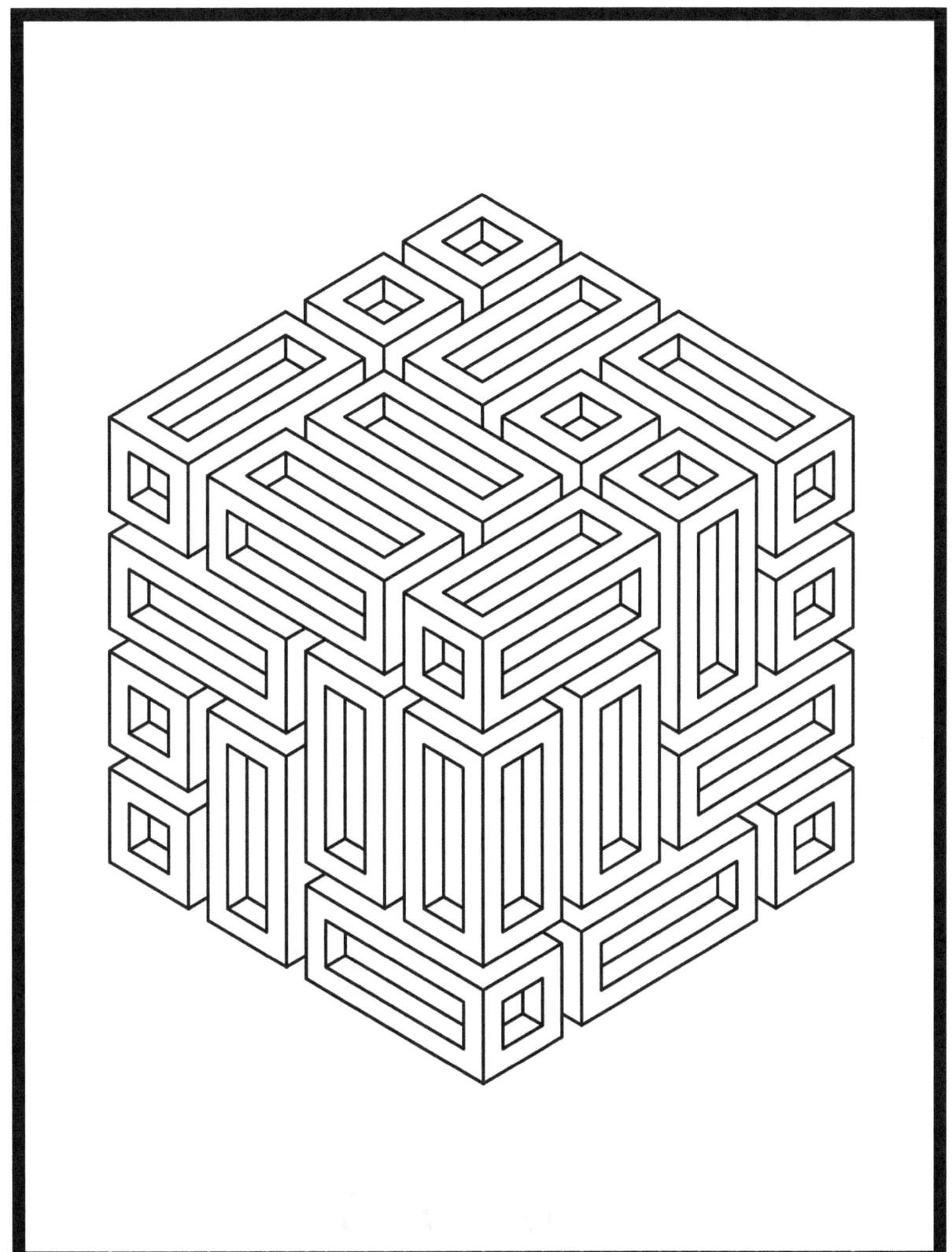

Cube No. 9

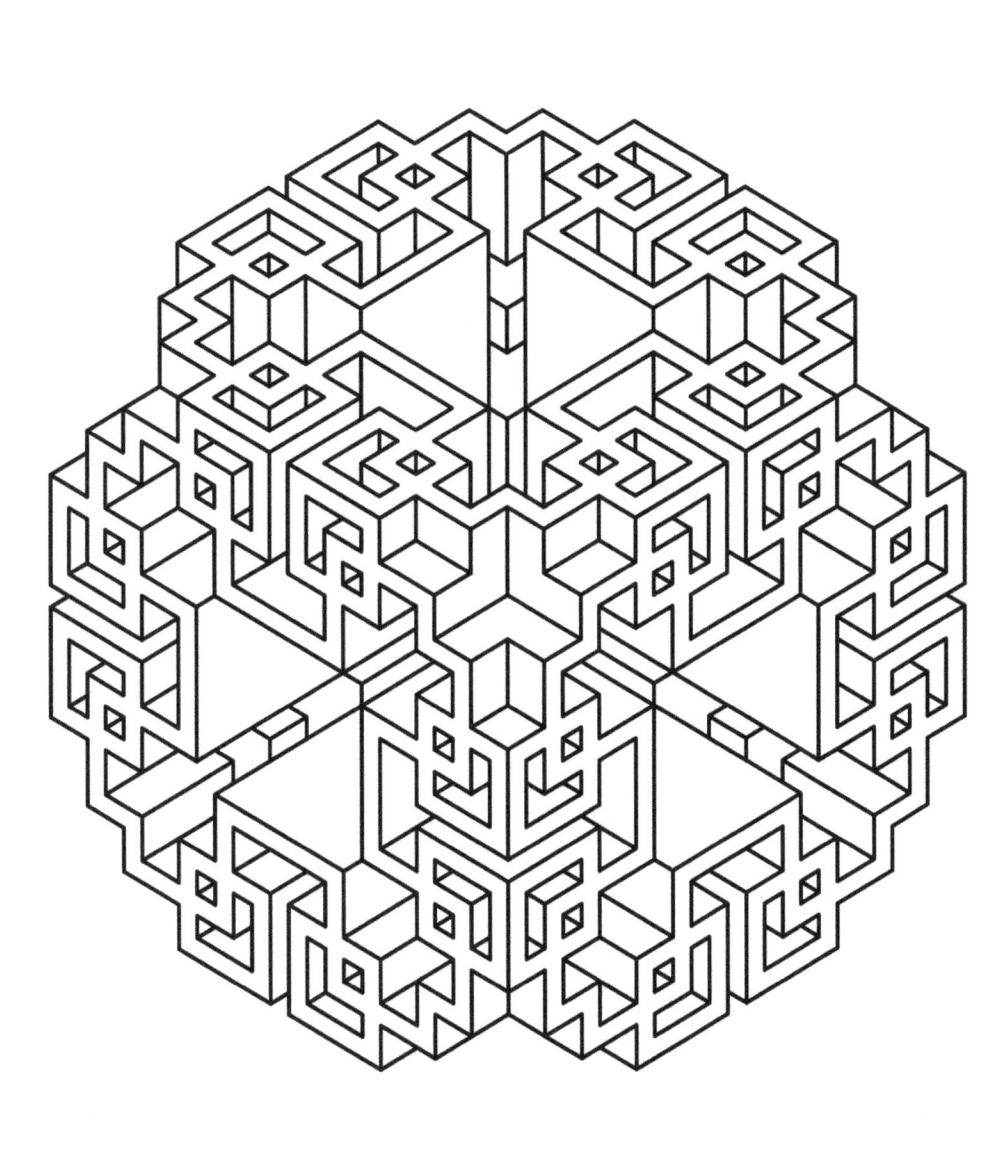

Cube No. 10

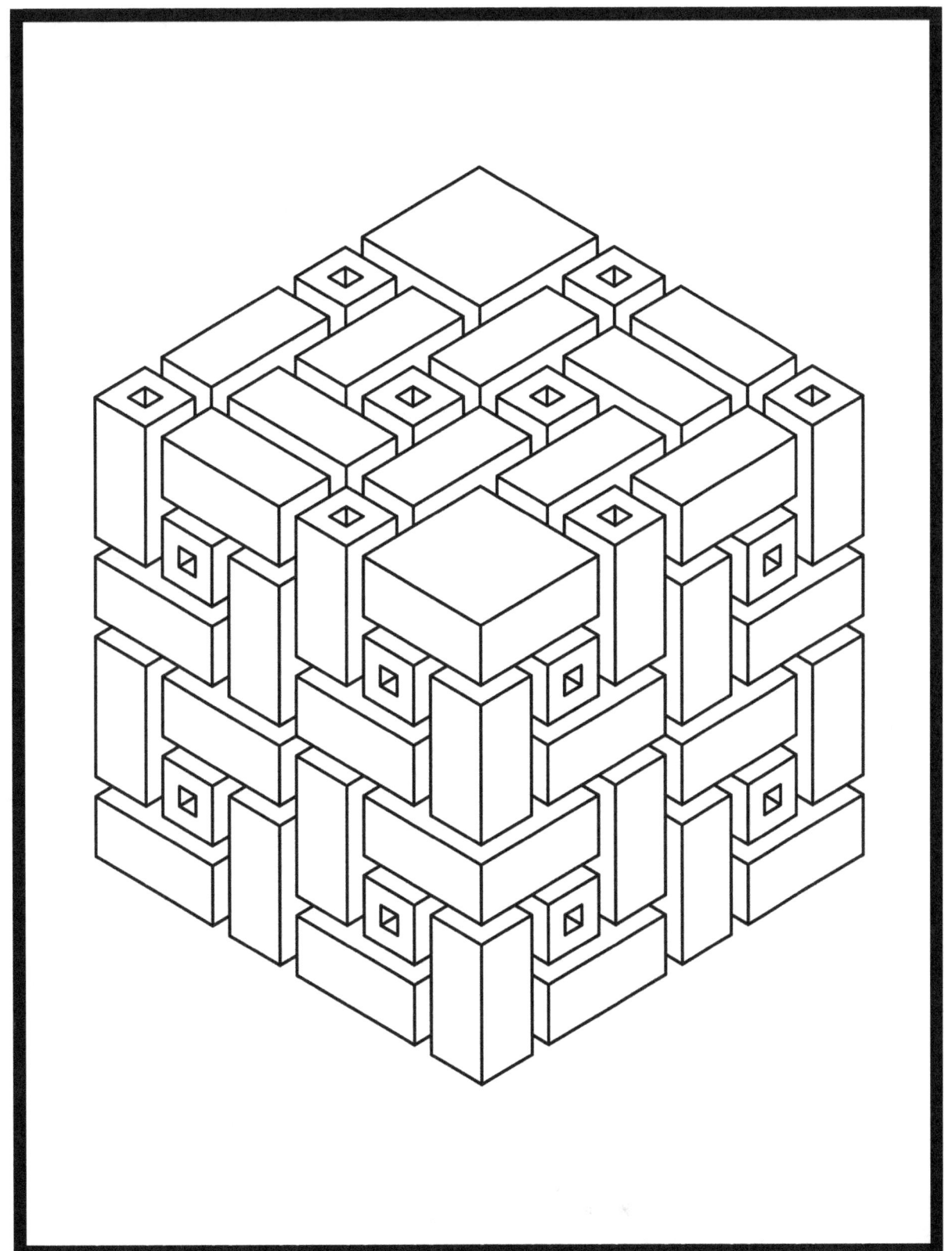

Cube No. 11

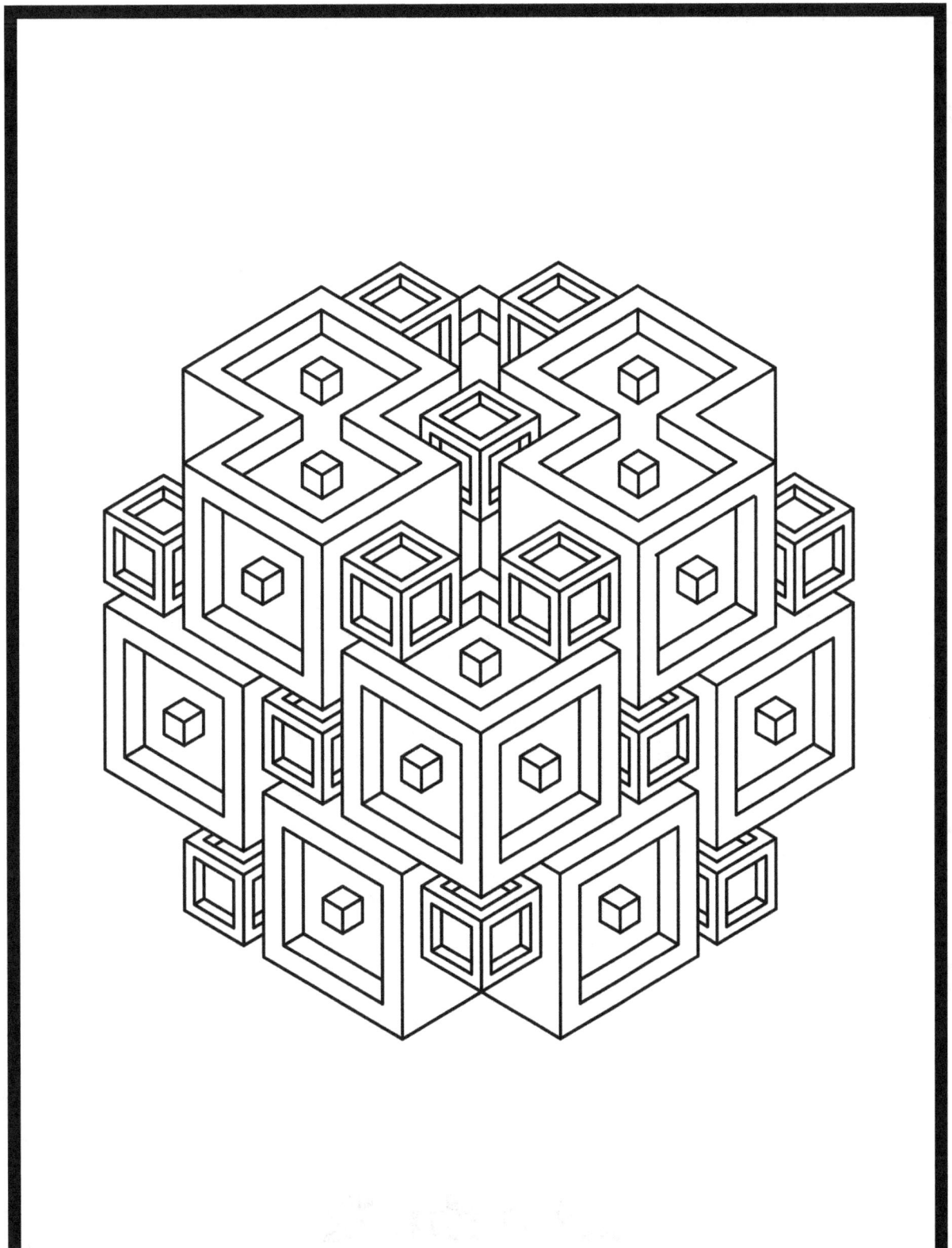

Cube No. 12

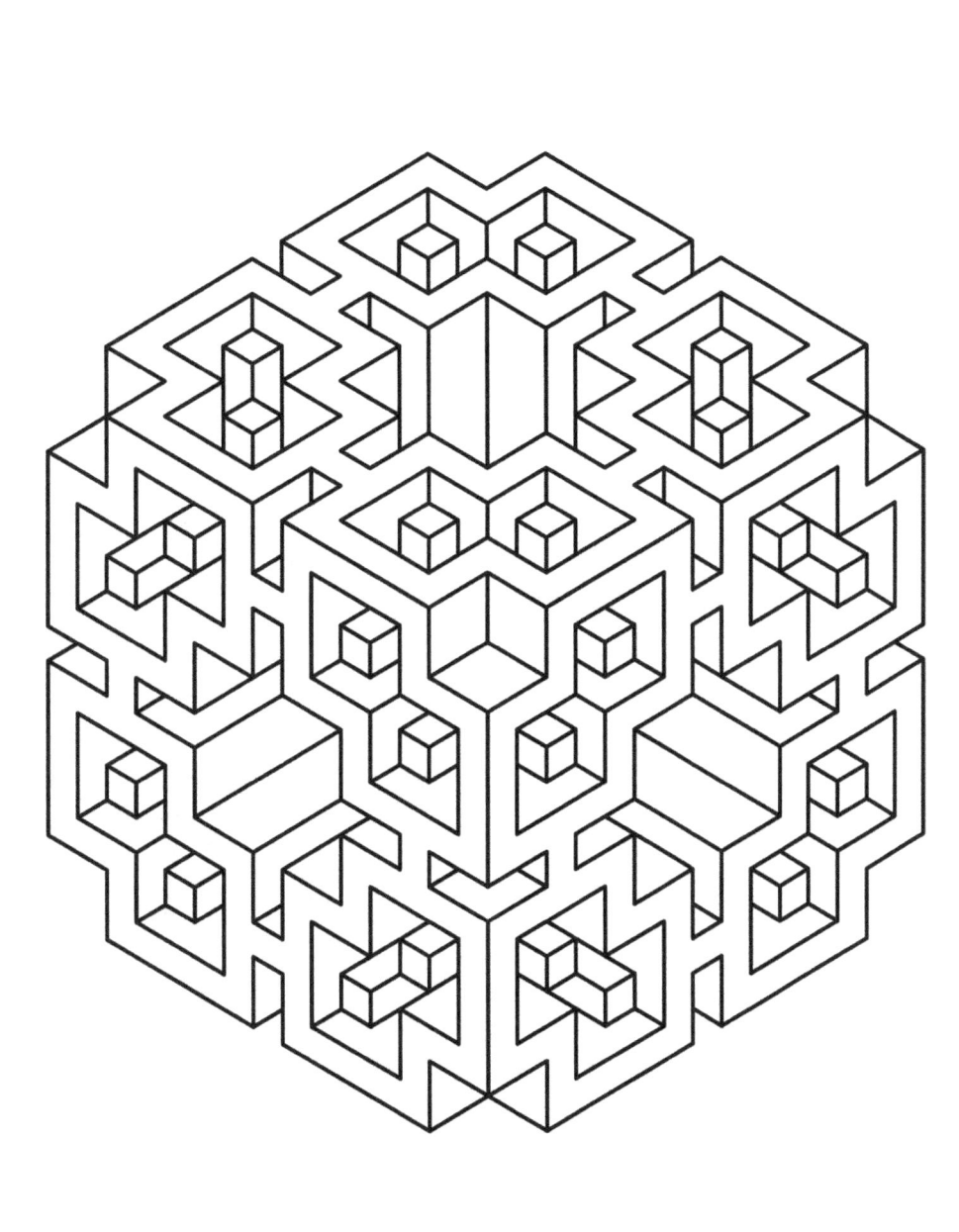

Cube No. 13

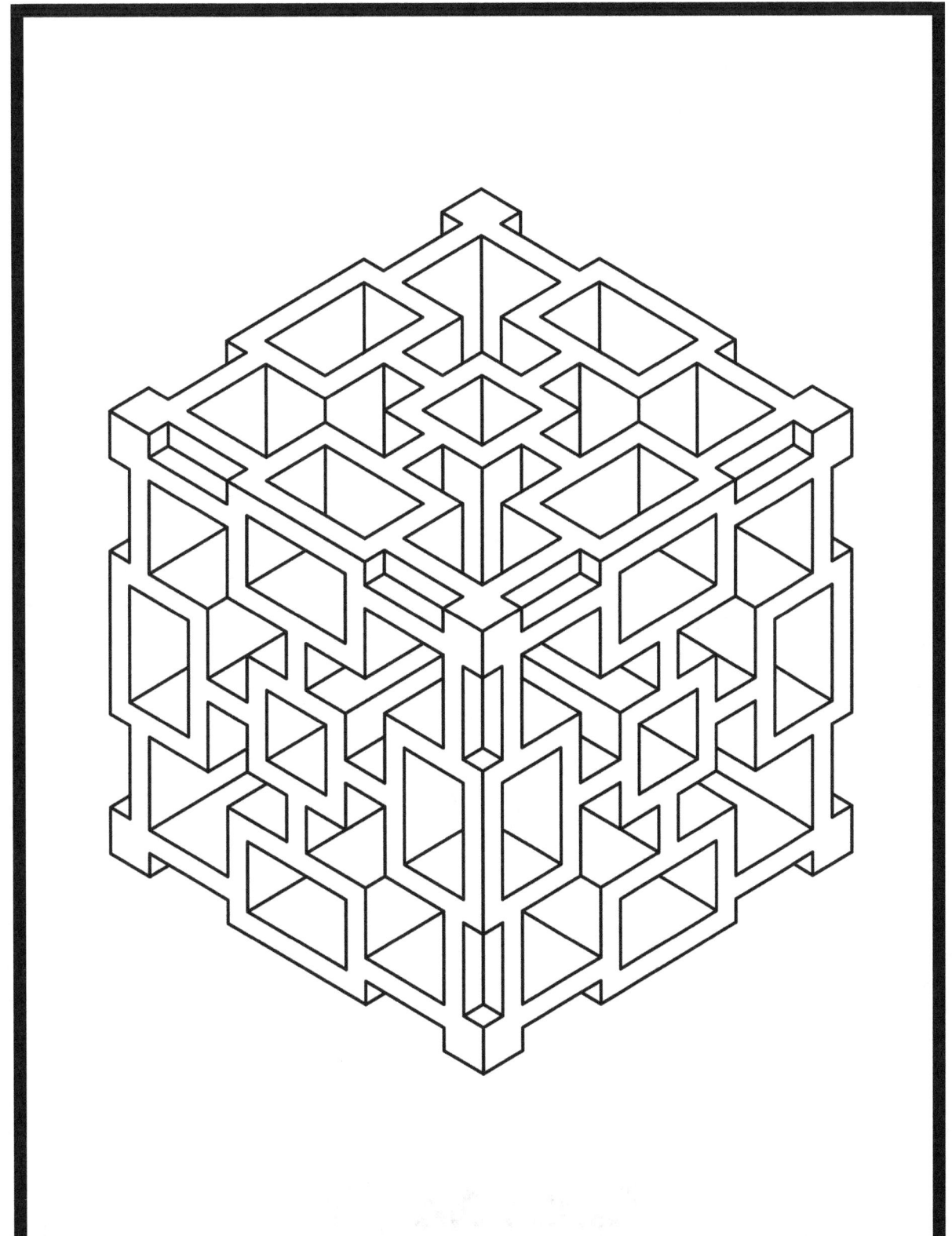

Cube No. 14

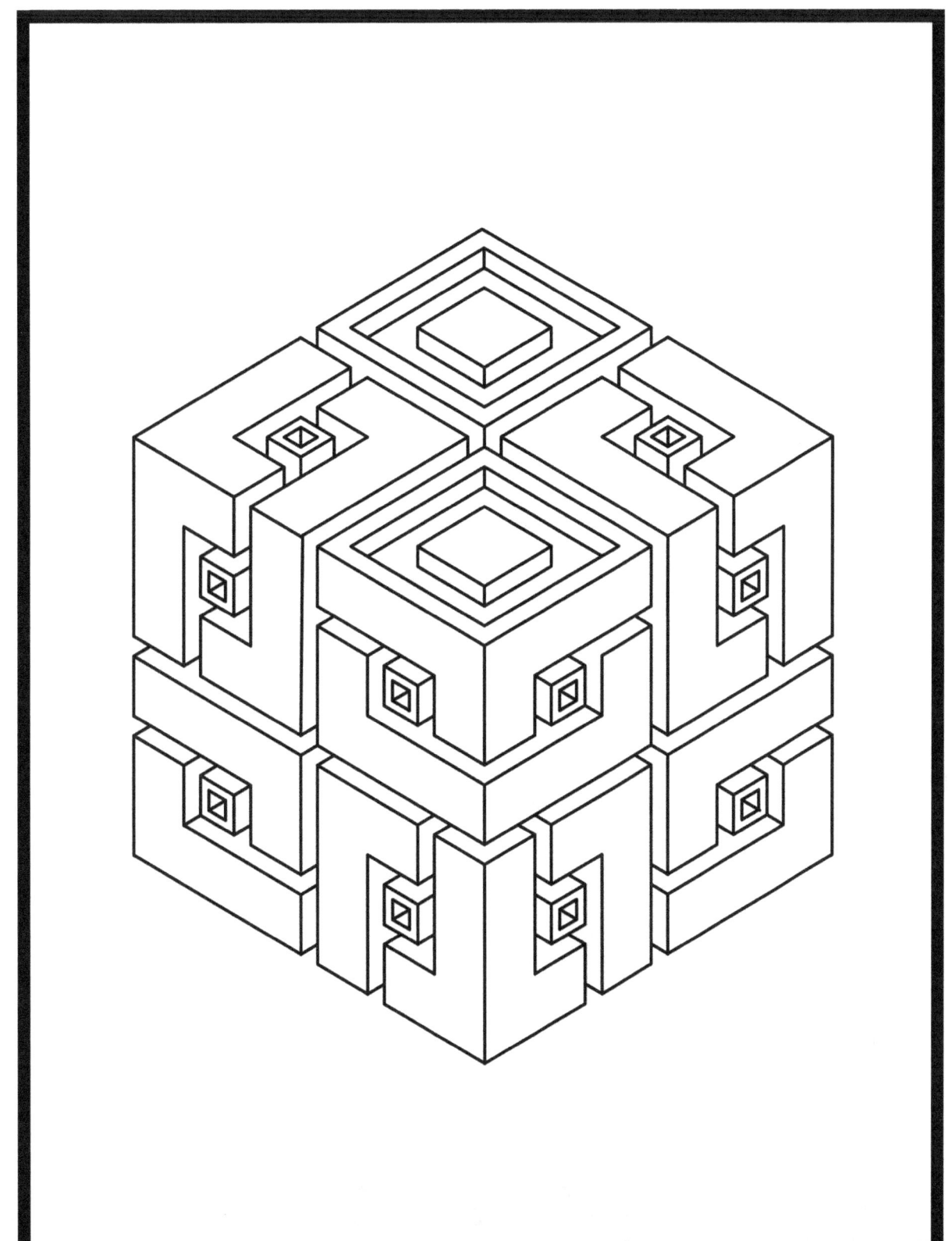

Cube No. 15

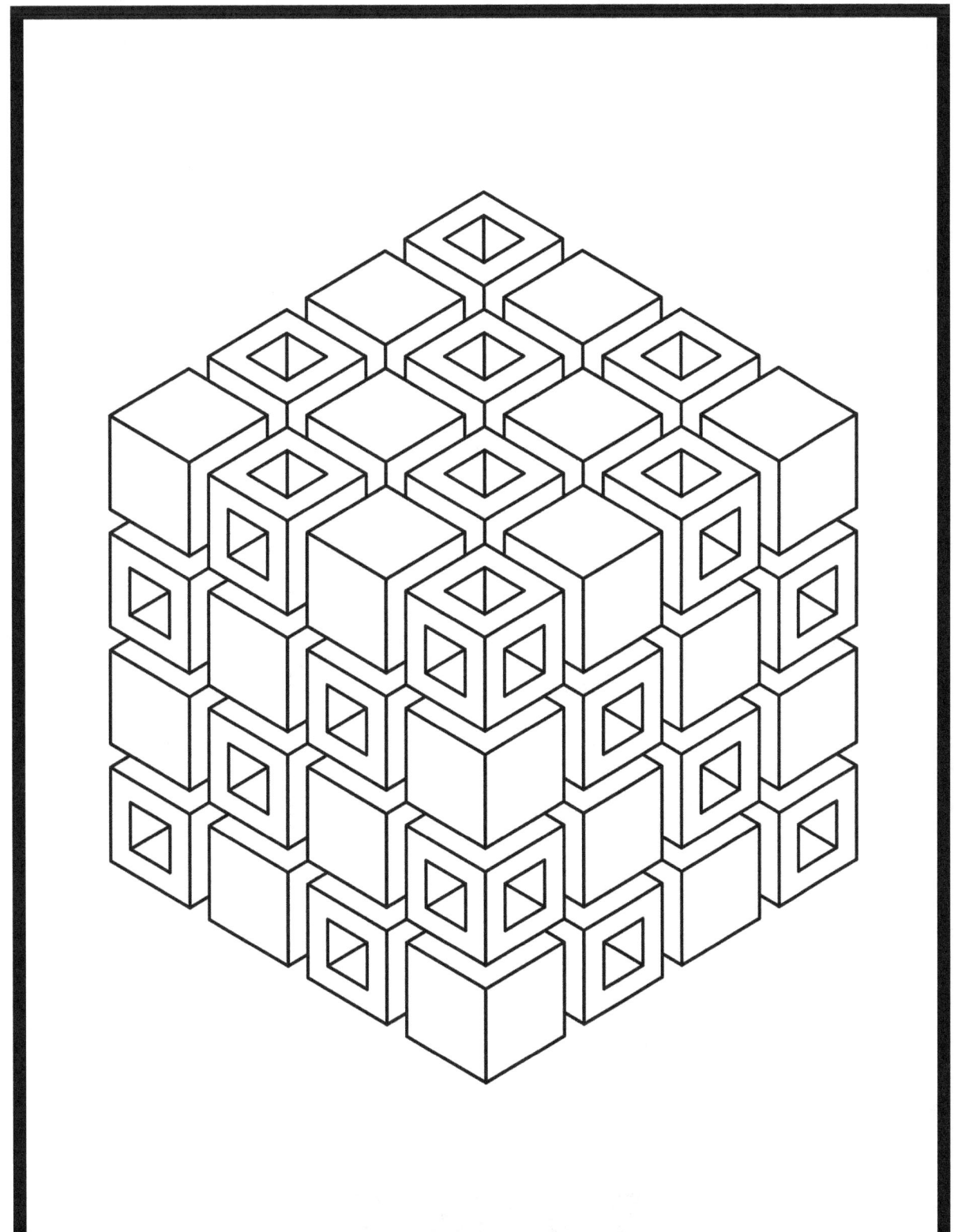

Cube No. 16

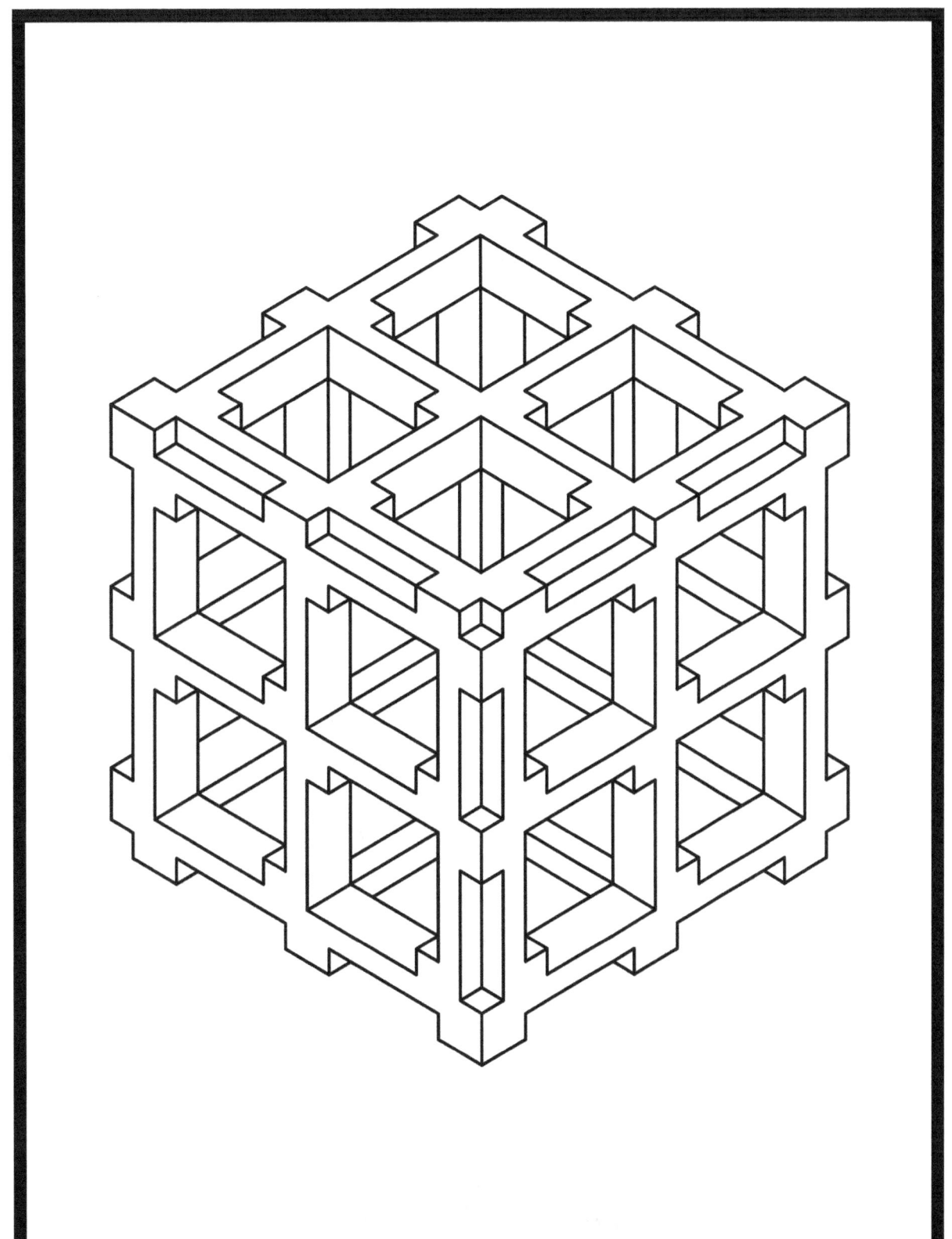

Cube No. 17

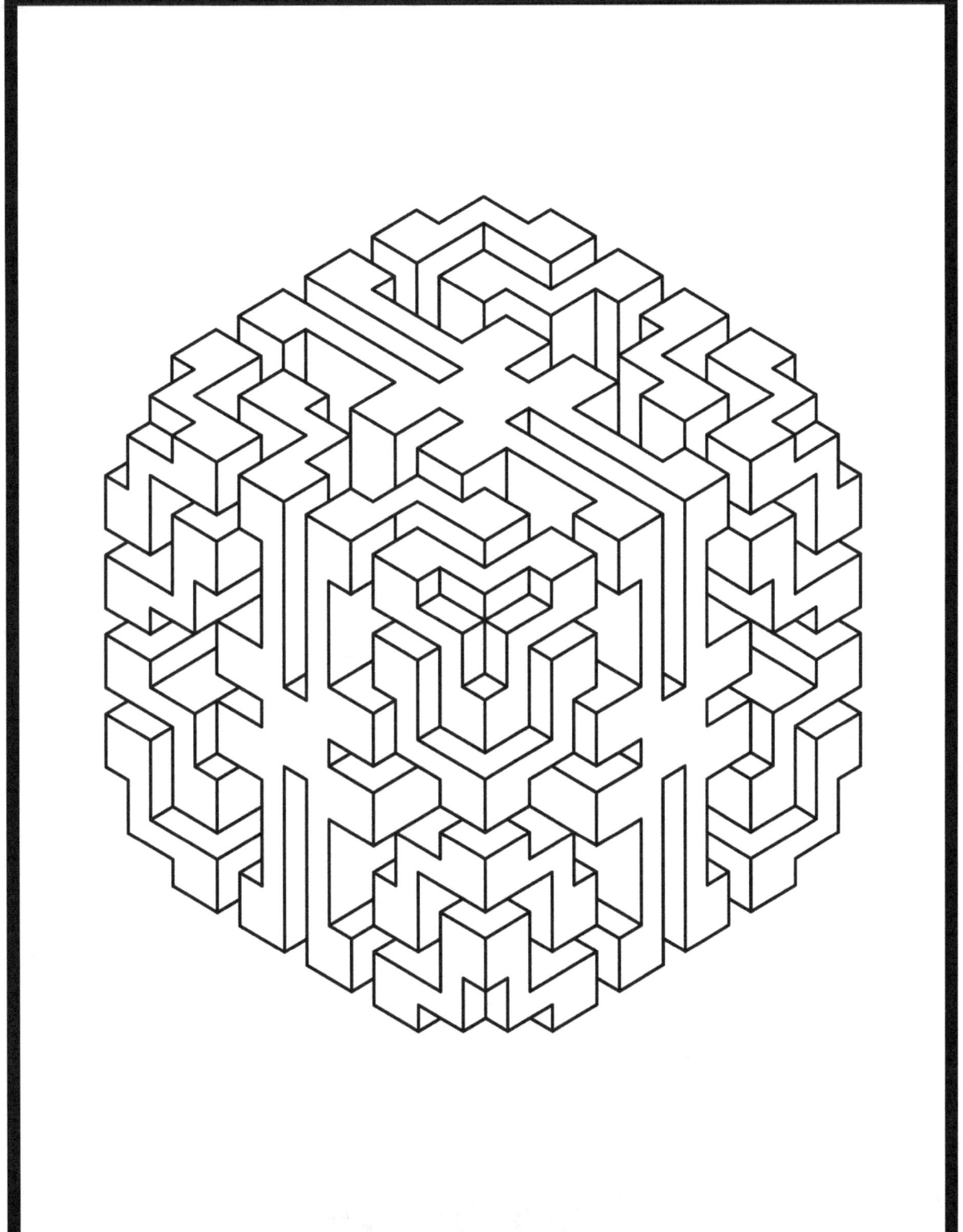

Cube No. 18

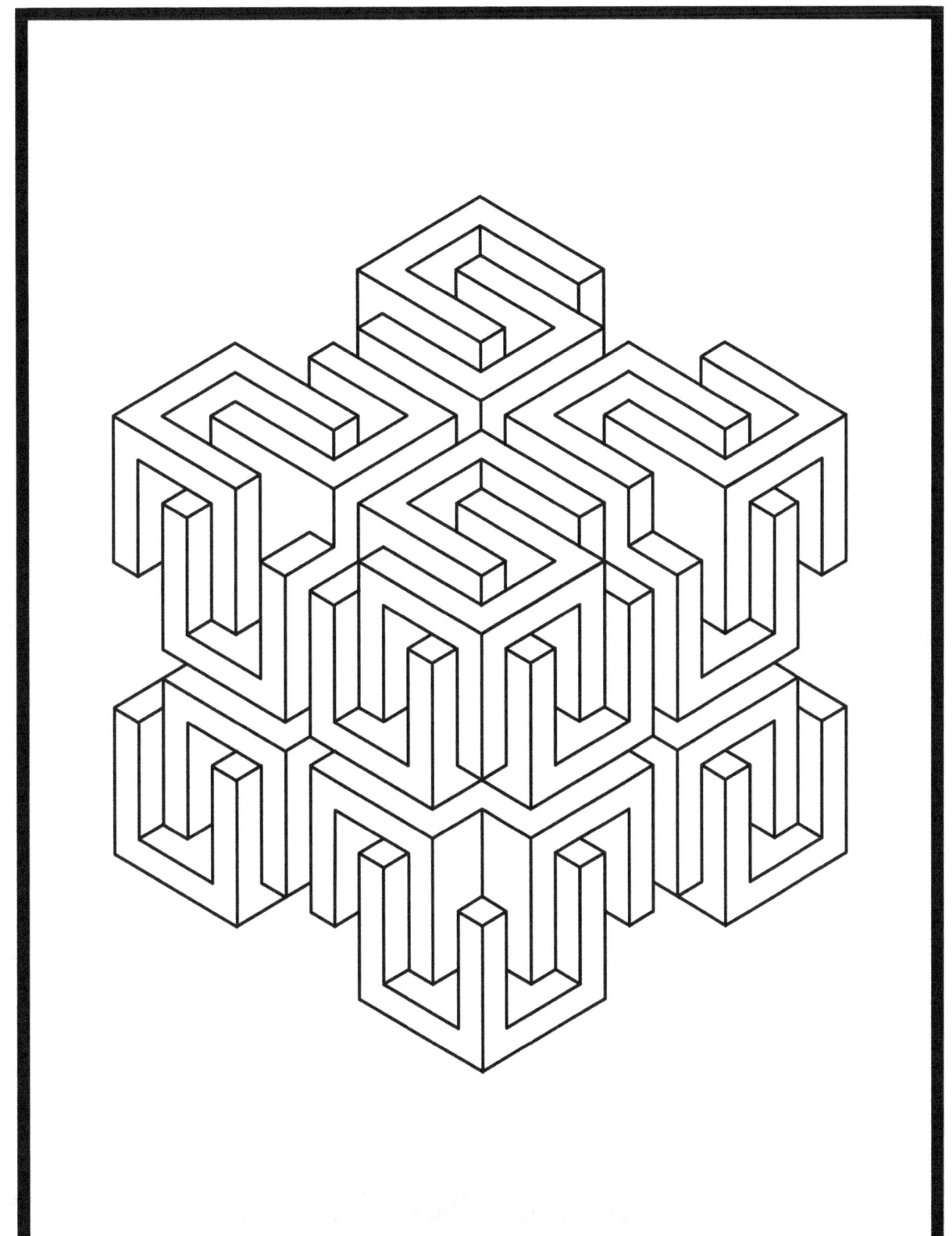

Cube No. 19

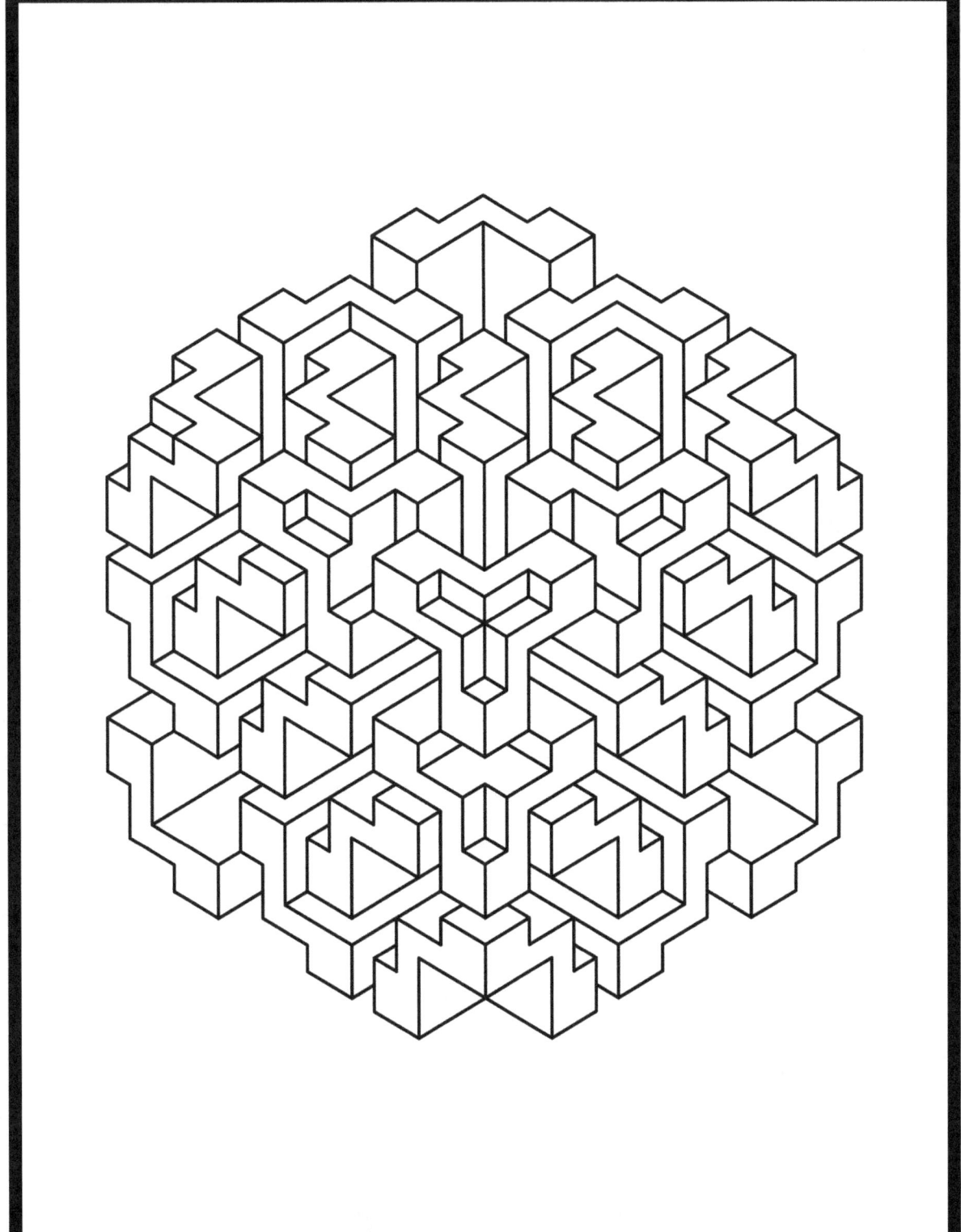

Cube No. 20

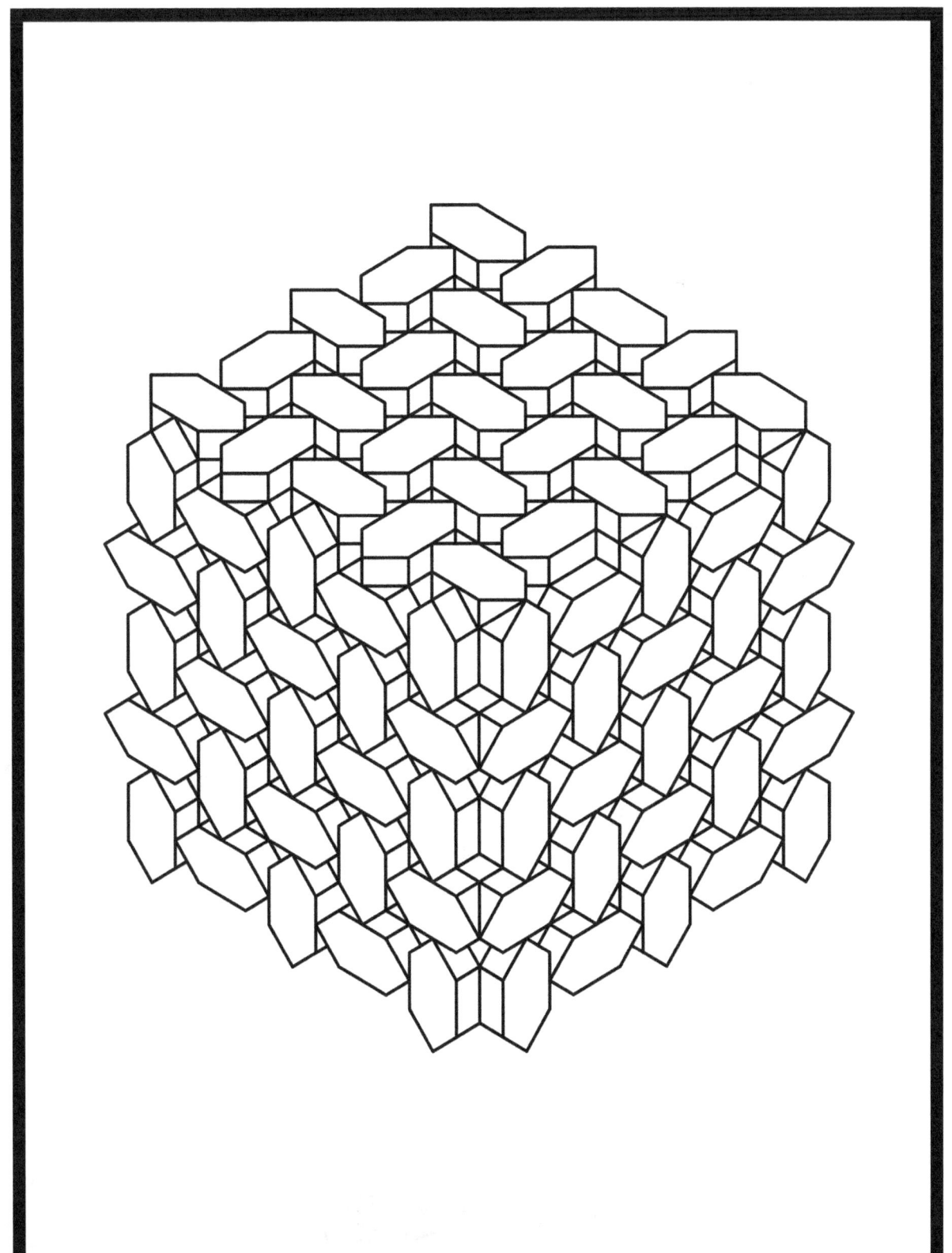

Cube No. 21

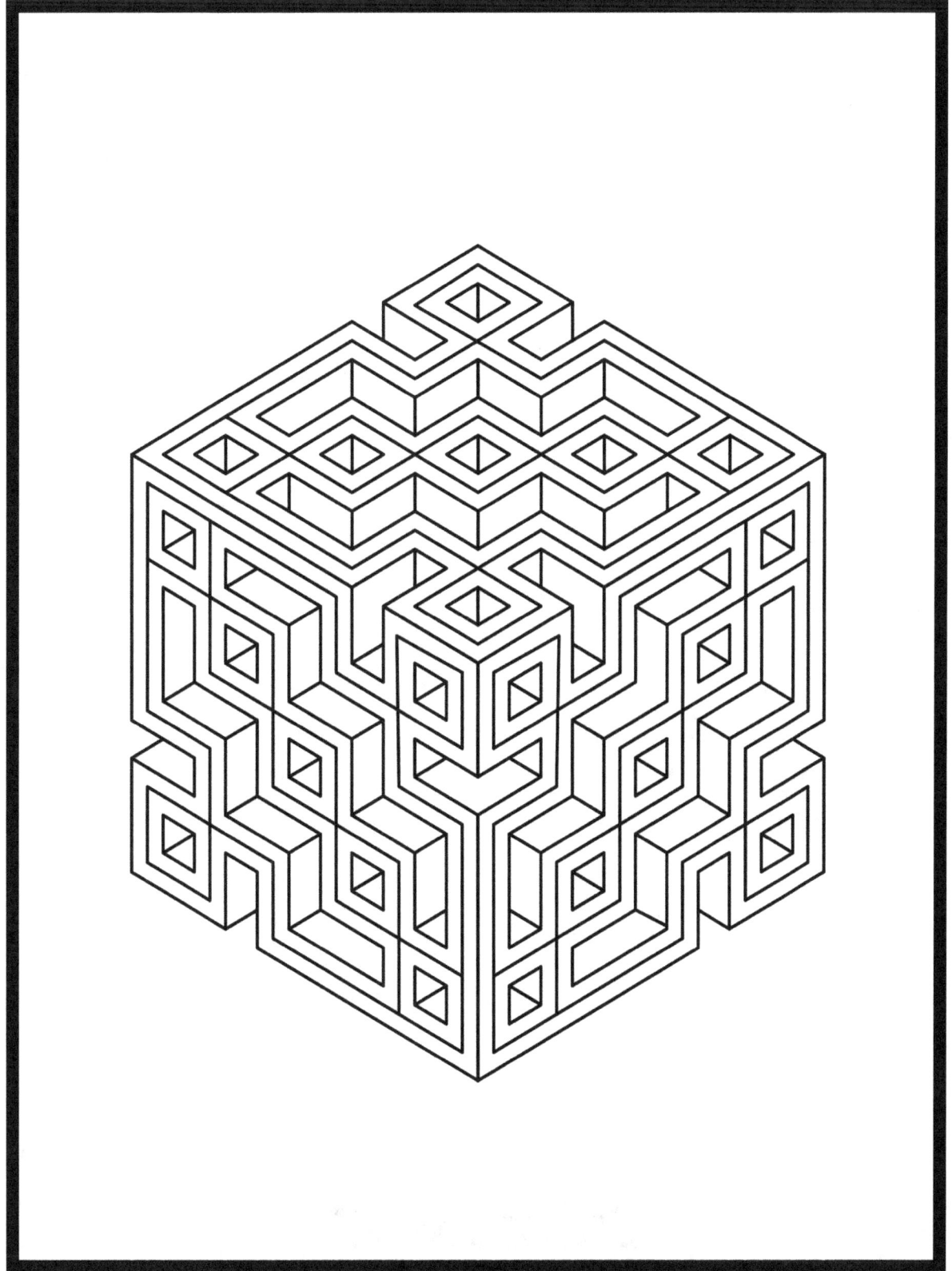

Cube No. 22

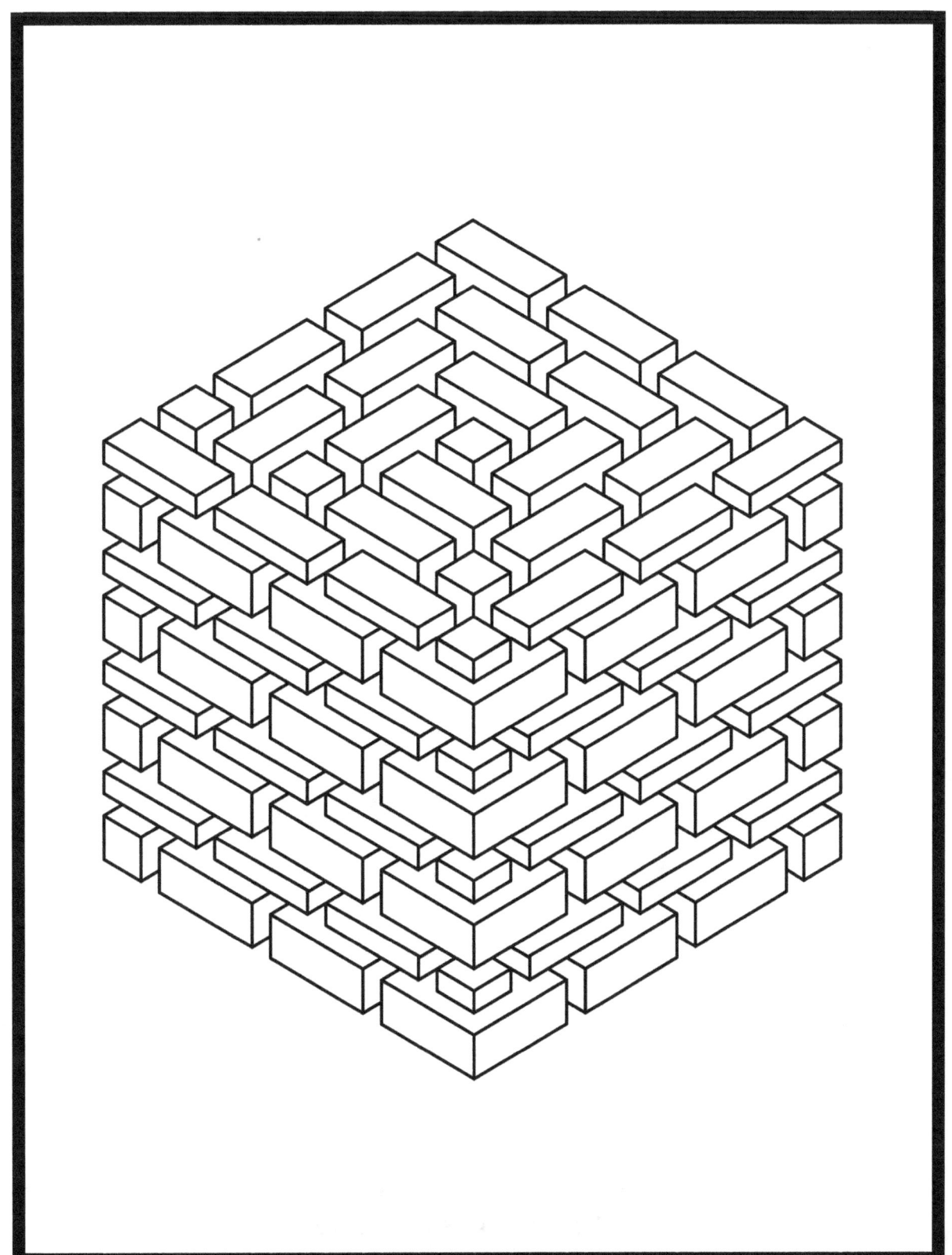

Cube No. 23

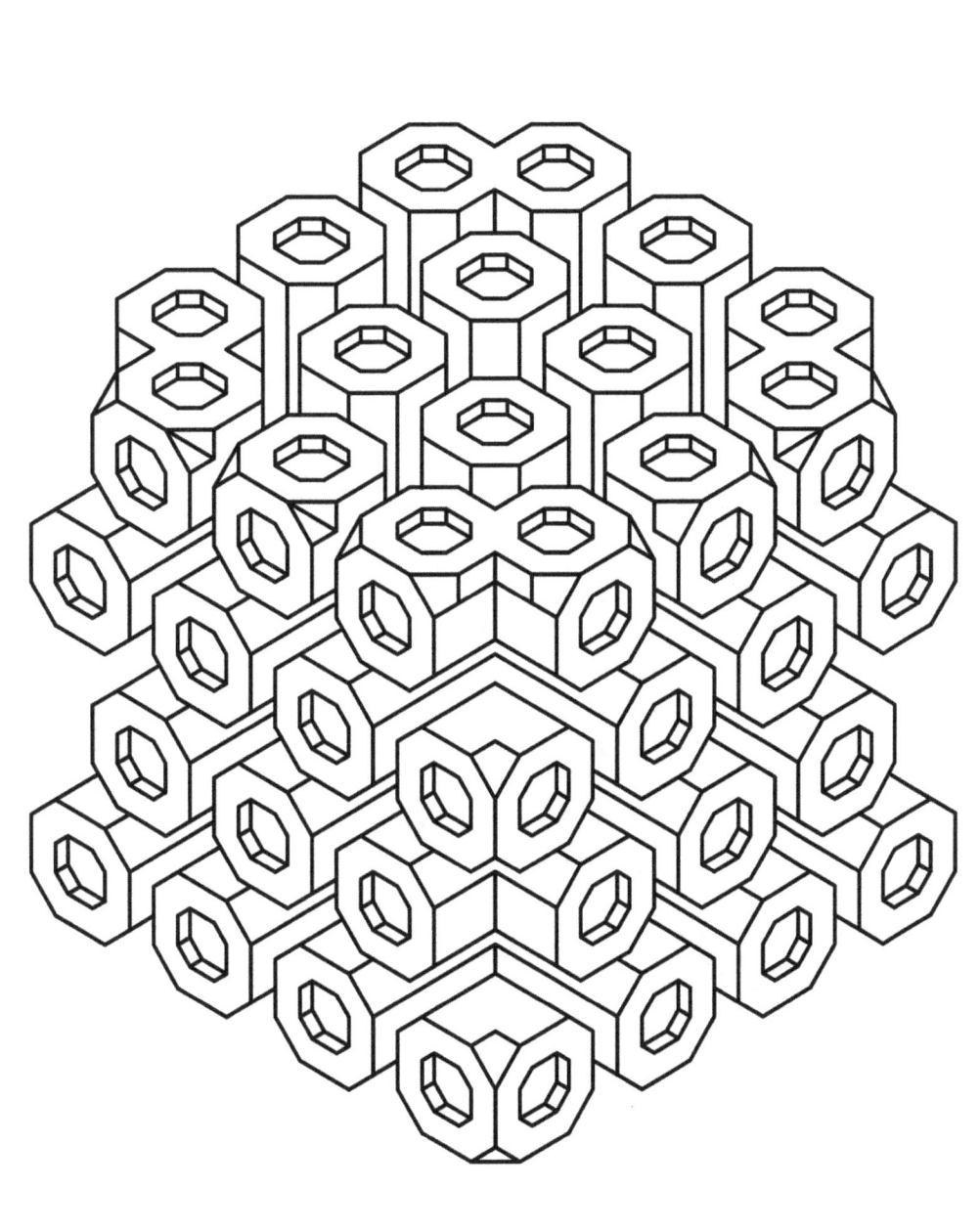

Cube No. 24

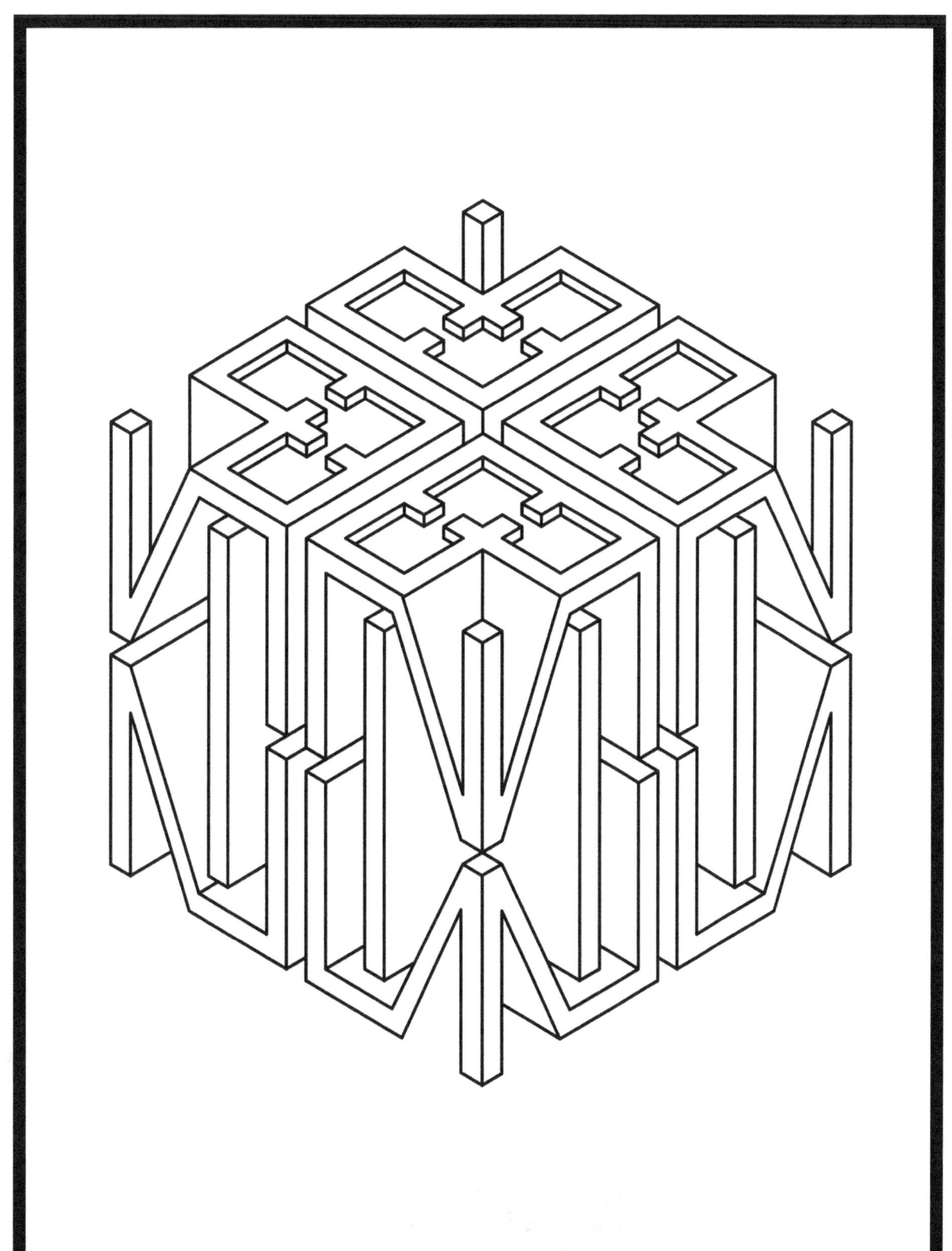

Cube No. 25

www.ingramcontent.com/pod-product-compliance
Lightning Source LLC
Chambersburg PA
CBHW080535220526
45465CB00006B/2716